THE
BEST
EVER
JOBS
IN

TECHNOLOGY

PAUL MASON

WAYLAND

First published in Great Britain
in 2020 by Wayland
Copyright © Hodder and Stoughton, 2020
All rights reserved

Series editor: Amy Pimperton
Produced by Tall Tree Ltd
Editor: Lara Murphy
Designer: Gary Hyde

HB ISBN: 978 1 5263 1300 3
PB ISBN: 978 1 5263 1301 0

Wayland
An imprint of Hachette Children's Group
Part of Hodder and Stoughton
Carmelite House
50 Victoria Embankment
London EC4Y 0DZ

An Hachette UK Company
www.hachette.co.uk
www.hachettechildrens.co.uk

Printed and bound in China

Picture Credits

t-top, b-bottom, l-left, r-right, c-centre, front cover-fc, back cover - bc
3tr, 22 all, 23t shutterstock/sivVector, 3ctl, 13tr and cl shutterstock/Vector Tradition, 3cl, 39tr shutterstock/Salim Nasirov, 3br, 20bl shutterstock, 4cl shutterstock/ SmileStudio, bl shutterstock/ Evgeny Turaev, 5tr, 34c shutterstock/Khomenko Serhii, cl, 19 tl, br, 46tr shutterstock/ NastyaSigne, br shutterstock/ aliaksei kruhlenia, 6cl shutterstock/ctrlaplus, bl shutterstock/VikiVector, 7t shutterstock/george photo cm, b shutterstock/ProStockStudio, 8bl shutterstock/WEI LING CHANG, 9cl shutterstock./Iconic Bestiary, cr shutterstock/ Elegant Solution, bl shutterstock/Alberto Loyo, 10br shutterstock/Sailor Johnny, 11tl shutterstock/Kluva, b shutterstock/fizkes, 12b shutterstock/Arkadivna, 13cr shutterstock/ art_cathryn, b Los Angeles Examiner/USC Libraries/Corbis via Getty Images, 14cl and 15tl shutterstock/ VikiVector, bl shutterstock/metamorworks, 15cl shutterstock/Svetlana Maslova, 16cr shutterstock/Marcin Balcerzak, br shutterstock/Shipov Oleg, 17tl shutterstock/FARBAI, 17cr shutterstock/pang_oasis, 18 shutterstock/volkanakmese, 19 br Mimmo Frassineti/Agf/Shutterstock, 21t shutterstock/Sk Hasan Ali, br shutterstock/Denys Po, 23b NASA/James Blair, 24l shutterstock/Nagajadon, 25tr shutterstock/Vectorpocket, b shutterstock/Radu Razvan, 26r shutterstock/Macrovector, 27t shutterstock/BigMouse, b shutterstock/homydesign, 28cr shutterstock/Isaac Marzioli, b shutterstock/Magicleaf, 29tr shutterstock/olllikeballoon, c shutterstock/vectorpouch, b shutterstock/Marco Canoniero, 30cr shutterstock/Diamond_Images, b shutterstock/Deena Summers, 31tl shutterstock/ Malachi Jacobs, cr shutterstock/galimovma79, cl shutterstock/Richard Thornton, 32b shutterstock/Action Sports Photography, 33t shutterstock/Oskar SCHULER, cr shutterstock/ Hafiz Johari, cr shutterstock/Martial Red, 34b shutterstock, 35tr shutterstock/Rvector, cr shutterstock/Golden Sikorka, b shutterstock/Sunshine Seeds, 36cr and br shutterstock/ Melok, bl shutterstock/trgrowth, 37tl shutterstock/Djohan Shahrin, b shutterstock/ Tinseltown, 38cr shutterstock/Daniel Wiedemann, br shutterstock/Maksbart, 39r shutterstock/Dmitry Kalinovsky, 40 all, 47br shutterstock/arturick, 41tl shutterstock/ bigredlynx, tr shutterstock/Tarzhanova, bl shutterstock/LanKogal, 42bl shutterstock/Lal Perera, br shutterstock/GoodStudio, 43tl, 48b shutterstock/Yaroslav Shkuro, cr shutterstock/ JesO, b both courtesy of Library of Congress, 44cr, 48t shutterstock/Zoart Studio, b shutterstock/GraphicsRF, 45cr shutterstock/natnatnat

MIX
Paper from
responsible sources
FSC® C104740
www.fsc.org

Contents

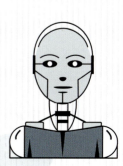

Top technology jobs

Many technology jobs are all about complicated electronics or programming computers to do clever things, but there are lots of other jobs in the tech world, too. Technology is scientific knowledge used for practical things – for example, making useful tools and improved products. Our world relies on technology in millions of ways and the number of tech jobs out there is staggering!

SPORTS

The world of sport is full of tech. In motorsports, computer engineers work out aerodynamic designs, tyre designers develop new, grippier technology and engineers make the engines as powerful as possible. In mountaineering, technology keeps climbers alive in places without enough oxygen for survival. In football, technology makes boots that kick more accurately and goalie gloves that hold the ball better.

FILMS

Technology is crucial in film-making. It is used for everything from recording sound to the actual filming, special effects and finally turning all the separate bits into a film that makes sense.

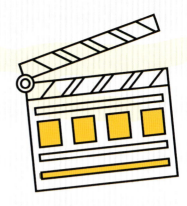

MEDICINE

Technology helps us to discover what is wrong with people and then is used to cure them. Hi-tech machines, such as CT scanners, need operators who can work the technology. But medicine also has more hands-on tech jobs: imagine designing and making an artificial limb for someone who then uses it to run a marathon or climb a mountain.

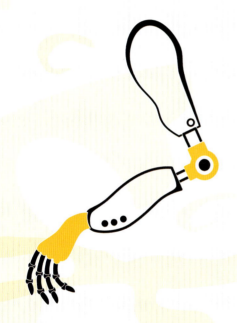

ALL AROUND US

Almost everything around us has a technology-related job linked to it. The homes we live in are designed by architects using the latest technology. Our cars, bicycles, scooters, skateboards, clothes and even food are all produced using new technology.

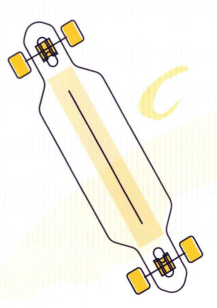

Architect

Have you ever spent time doodling on some graph paper, designing your dream treehouse, cabin, football stadium or skyscraper? If so, it might just be that inside you there's an architect itching to get out.

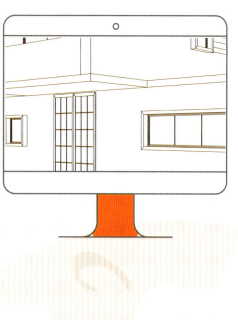

TECH WIZARDS

Architects have to constantly keep up with the latest technologies. These include CAD systems for designing buildings and other structures on screen. They can be used to test designs before they are actually built. An architect also has to understand the technologies used in construction. Whether they are designing a home loft extension or a state-of-the-art sports stadium, knowing the strongest, lightest materials or most sustainable heating and cooling systems is crucial.

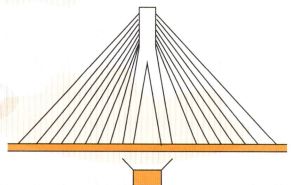

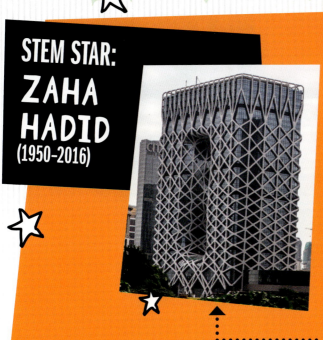

Hadid's best-known project may be the London Olympics Aquatic Centre, completed in 2011. The roof featured the curving shape that Hadid's designs are famous for. Two huge spectator areas with an extra 14,700 seats were added for the Games, then dismantled and sold or recycled. The Morpheus Hotel in Macau is a completely different building with a steel exoskeleton and curving shapes carved into its core.

The Morpheus Hotel was finished after Hadid's death.

A WORLD OF ARCHITECTURE

As an architect, you might work on a wide variety of buildings, from modern skyscrapers to ancient manor houses, tiny apartments, hotels and everyday houses. You have to enjoy a challenge: can you design what your client wants at a price they can afford to pay? Most architects work on all sorts of projects, but some become famous for designing particular types of structure. Santiago Calatrava, for example, is best known for designing bridges and passenger terminals at train stations and airports.

Behind the scenes: Celebrity architects

Most architects work on ordinary buildings, because there are a lot of these around. A few, though, are famous for the world's biggest construction projects. These celebrity architects might design anything from huge skyscrapers to train stations, tunnels or bridges.

VINCENT CALLEBAUT

Callebaut designs futuristic eco-projects that often include plants as part of the design. His designs include a holiday resort in the Philippines that produces no gases that would harm the environment and no waste. His Agora Tower, or Tao Zhu Yin Yuan, in Taipei, Taiwan, is designed to get its energy from sunlight and is constructed using a mixture of recycled and recyclable materials.

The Agora Tower's design is based on the double helix shape of DNA.

HERZOG & DE MEURON

Jacques Herzog and Pierre de Meuron are most famous for their work on the old Bankside Power Station beside the River Thames in London. In 2000 they converted it into Tate Modern, now one of the most famous art galleries in the city. One of their most recent projects is the Tai Kwun Centre for Heritage and Art in the middle of Hong Kong. This was a police station, prison and court building that has been turned into an arts centre.

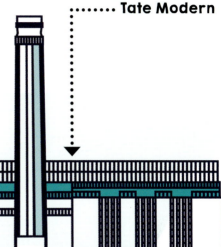

········· **Tate Modern**

STEM STAR: FRANK GEHRY
(1929–)

Frank Gehry is one of the world's most famous architects. As a boy he played at designing miniature cities on the living-room floor, using blocks of wood from his granddad's hardware store. After first working as a truck driver, Gehry studied architecture. Today, he is best known for his silver-clad buildings, which look as though they are covered in fish scales.

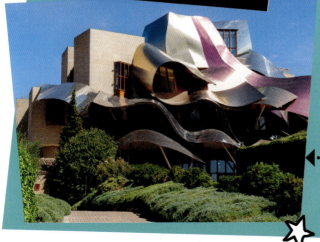

The Marqués de Riscal hotel in Spain, was designed by Gehry.

App developer

Imagine if every time your friends used their phone, they opened an app you had written? If that sounds like a cool thing, maybe you should think about becoming an app developer.

DO YOU SPEAK COMPUTER?

To be an app developer you'll have to be able to write computer code: instructions that tell a computer what to do. Code is written in programming languages and to be an app developer, you need to understand at least one of these languages. There are hundreds, but the most common are JavaScript, Swift, Java, C++ and Python. Java and Python are among the easiest computer programming languages for beginners to learn.

ALL KINDS OF APPS

For many people apps are a vital part of their lives, so there is almost no limit to the kinds of app you could develop. There are sports apps, shopping apps, news apps and diary apps. There are even apps that tell you when to go to sleep and wake up. Apps are developed because a person or company has identified something people want or need, such as listening to podcasts or reviews of video games. As an app developer, your job is to write a piece of computer software that will help them do this.

TRAINING:
DEVELOPING THE DEVELOPERS

Computer technology changes very quickly, so app developers have to keep learning new skills. Some become experts in particular kinds of information technology, such as databases. Others try to know as much as possible about just one language, such as the C++ language used by many graphics and games developers.

▲
⋮....... Students learning coding skills with the help of a tutor

Furniture designer

Do you have a chair you hate sitting in because it is uncomfortable, or maybe a table your legs won't fit underneath properly? If you think you could have made a better version yourself, how about becoming a furniture designer?

LAYERS OF TECHNOLOGY

Modern furniture designers use all kinds of technology. They may sketch their first designs on a piece of paper, but it will soon be put on screen in a CAD design. They use biometrics to work out the size and shape of design, so that it will be comfortable for the maximum range of shapes and sizes of people. The CAD design is used to make precise instructions for the factory that will make the furniture, so that all the parts fit together perfectly.

DESIGN WORLD

As a furniture designer you could end up doing all kinds of work. Some designers work for themselves, making small numbers of items in a traditional way. They hope to sell these for a high price. Others work for themselves but sell their designs to big companies, which will make thousands of copies. Big stores also employ their own full-time designers in their own design studios to create new products.

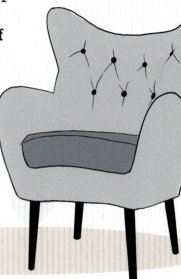

STEM STARS: CHARLES AND RAY EAMES
CHARLES (1907–1978)
RAY (1912–1988)

Charles and Ray (Ray was a woman: her actual name was Bernice Alexandra) Eames were architects and industrial designers in the USA. Among their products were plywood leg splints for Second World War (1939–45) soldiers, mass-produced dining chairs, and a famous lounge chair and footstool now famous as the 'Eames chair'.

Radiologist

If the idea of peering inside people's bodies (without cutting them open) appeals to you, becoming a radiologist could just be your dream tech job. Radiologists are doctors who help diagnose illnesses by taking images of patients' insides.

AMAZING MACHINES

Radiologists use some of the most-complicated machines in medicine. They have X-ray machines for taking two dimensional images. Far more complicated computed tomography (CT) scans take X-rays from different angles, then combine them to make a three-dimensional image. Radiologists also use fluoroscopy machines, which produce a kind of X-ray video. MRI scans use magnetic fields instead of X-rays, and ultrasound uses sound waves.

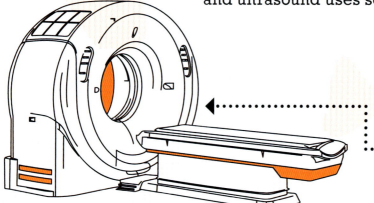

A CT scanner

DIAGNOSTICS AND SURGERY

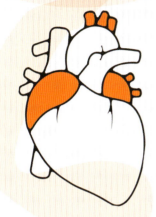

As a radiologist there are two main ways you'll be able to help people. The first is by diagnosing what is wrong with them. You might specialise in particular types of patient: children, people with joint or bone problems or heart patients. The second area of radiology is linked to keyhole surgery. In this, a radiologist guides the surgery so that it solves the problem with as little damage to the rest of the body as possible.

STEM STAR: WILHELM RÖNTGEN (1845–1923)

Röntgen was a physicist not a doctor, but he is often described as the founder of radiology. In the 1890s he discovered X-rays (which at the time were sometimes called Röntgen rays). His first image was a ghostly skeleton of his own body; the first permanent X-ray was of the bones inside his wife's hand.

Behind the scenes: Radiology in action

These three case studies* show some of the ways in which, as a real-life radiologist, you could help diagnose and treat people's health problems.

CASE STUDY 1: 'IT HURTS TO WEE'

A four-year-old girl tells her mum that it hurts to wee. In fact, it has been hurting for days, but she was embarrassed to say. Their family doctor says they need to go to hospital for an ultrasound examination. In this, a radiologist uses sound waves to form images of the girl's kidneys and bladder. They show that she has an infection in her bladder – which can easily be treated with antibiotics.

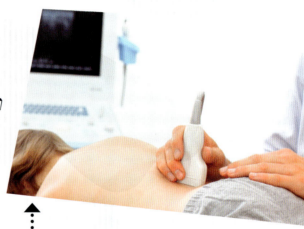

....Using an ultrasound machine to scan a patient's kidneys

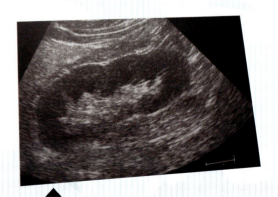

An ultrasound image of a kidney ....

CASE STUDY 2: 'MY SHOULDER HURTS'

A top competitive swimmer starts to get pain in his shoulder. His doctor says that the joint has become inflamed: injecting a drug called corticosteroid will stop the inflammation and pain. But the shoulder joint is very small and the injection has to be in exactly the right place. A specialist uses an ultrasound machine to see inside the swimmer's shoulder as the needle goes in. This makes sure the drugs are delivered to exactly the right place.

CASE STUDY 3: KILLING OFF CANCER

Cancer is a disease that causes harmful cells to grow into a tumour, or lump, inside the body. A patient with cancer can be helped by radiologists in three ways. First, they use imaging technology to discover exactly where the cancer is. The radiologist might even place a marker on it – a tiny piece of gold, perhaps, that will show up well on later X-rays. Second, radiation can be beamed at the cancer cells to kill them. Thirdly, the treatment can be guided to the exact-right place by imaging devices, such as mini-CT scanners.

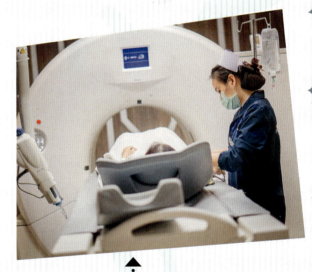

..... A nurse prepares a patient for a CT scan.

*The case studies are based on the kind of work radiologists do, but are not of real patients.

17

Prosthetics designer

If you love designing and making useful tools and want to make a big difference to the lives of people who have disabilities, becoming a prosthetics designer would be a great job.

BUILDING BODY PARTS

Prosthetics are artificial body parts, such as artificial hands, arms, feet and legs. As a designer, you will be working with lots of different technology. Most prosthetics are made specifically for their owner. The design is done on computer, using digital imaging, CAD and CAM software. You will need to understand the different materials used, such as plastic, leather, metal and carbon fibre. You might work with miniature electronics and the computers that control them.

While early prosthetics were basic, ...➤ such as wooden legs, modern versions are designed to mimic the actions of a normal living body part.

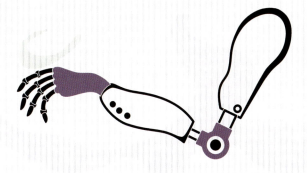

FROM ATHLETES TO COOKS ... AND MORE

You could end up designing prosthetics for all kinds of people and uses. Some para-athletes use carbon-fibre 'blades' when running. An ex-soldier who has lost a hand may want a hand/paddle so they can go surfing. Someone who is a keen cook might want a prosthetic that makes it easy to hold a bowl, whisk or knife.

STEM STAR: SOPHIE DE OLIVEIRA BARATA

Barata is a custom prosthetics designer from London. The limbs she designs combine usefulness with art. She designed a leg in the shape of a leg's muscles and bones, which the ex-soldier it was made for says is 'Awesome!' And the wearer of Barata's floral porcelain leg design said that, 'Having a beautifully crafted limb designed for you makes you feel special.'

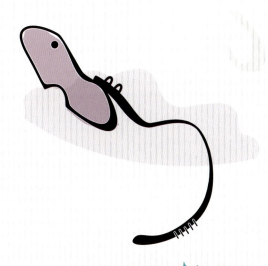

Barata's 'Stereo Leg'

Robot designer

Zeno, a robot shaped like a small cartoon boy, is being used to help children with autism learn how to communicate. If making a groundbreaking robot like this sounds like a good job, perhaps you should become a robot designer.

ROBOT EMOTIONS

Zeno's best feature is the way it can move its eyes, eyebrows and mouth to show emotions, such as happy, sad and angry. Practising these emotions with Zeno teaches autistic children how to show what they are feeling.

ROBOT TECH

You'll need to understand lots of different technologies to design a robot like Zeno. Your robot may have to be fitted with moving legs and arms, a camera, microphones, a speedometer and a compass. You may also need specialist computer software to control your robot's movements.

STEM STAR: DAVID HANSON
(1969–)

Hanson is the founder of Hanson Robotics, which builds the Zeno robot. His company also makes Einstein, Little Sophia and other robots. It was started in 2013 and is famous for making human-like robots. In 2017 Hanson's Sophia became the first robot ever to be given citizenship of a country – Saudi Arabia.

◀··· **Hanson and the** ····· **Sophia robot**

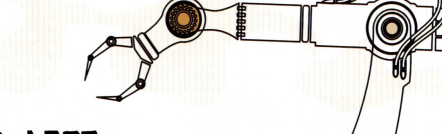

ROBO-LIFE

Tech experts have already developed robots that help humans in all kinds of ways. At home, some people use robot vacuum cleaners and lawnmowers. In places where there is conflict, robots defuse bombs. Manufacturing uses robots for welding, drilling, shaping and painting parts. As a robot designer, you could work in these areas or try new ones. Imagine building the first-ever robot goalkeeper or ice skater!

Space technician

Most people look at images of a rocket launch or the International Space Station and wonder what it would be like to be inside. If YOU think, 'I wonder how they built that?', maybe you should become a space technician.

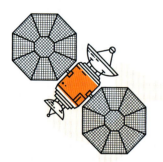

CUTTING-EDGE TECH

As a space technician you will use cutting-edge technologies to solve challenges. You might specialise in thermal technology: how do you stop a spacecraft's crew being frozen to death or burned to a crisp by extreme temperatures? Or you could work in energy systems: how could a space flight to Mars be powered? Or you might help develop a telescope that can see further into the Universe than ever before.

SPACE SPECIALIST

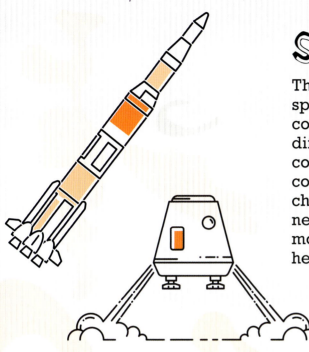

There are lots of different kinds of specialist space-technician jobs you could do. NASA, for example, hires 20 different kinds of engineer: the most common are aerospace, general and computer engineers. You will have a choice of whether to work developing new equipment, testing, building models or prototypes, or even helping to build an actual spacecraft.

TRAINING: NASA ENGINEERS

NASA trains its engineers using APPEL (Academy of Program/ Project & Engineering Leadership). APPEL suggests courses and new skills you could develop, depending on your job. For example, APPEL suggests Technical Engineers could go on a Creativity and Innovation course. It says their job's 'excessive focus on analysis, targets, and number crunching' may lead to them being less imaginative at work.

Race-bike designer

In some professional bike races, the cyclists cover over 3,000 kilometres before they reach the finish. The riders need the best bike possible – the lightest, fastest, most comfortable bike they can get – and this comes from their team's bike designers.

FROM CARBON TO AERODYNAMICS

As a bike designer, you have to understand all kinds of technology. First of all, most bikes are designed using CAD technology before a prototype is built. In a real-life race bike the materials technology includes carbon fibre (which almost all race bikes are made of), different kinds of metal and tyre rubber. You also need to understand aerodynamics, so that the bike will create as little air resistance as possible.

ALL TYPES OF BIKES

Of course, most people don't ride the kind of bike that wins races: those are a) expensive and b) uncomfortable. So as a bike designer you could work on all sorts of different designs, from mountain bikes that go downhill at death-defying speed to folding bikes for taking on trains. You might even end up manufacturing your own designs, after learning how on a frame-building course.

FAMOUS DESIGN:

LOOK

LOOK is a French bike company that was once a ski-binding manufacturer. It was the first to produce two modern bike technologies. First LOOK introduced clipless pedals, which allowed the rider to attach his or her shoes to the pedals (like a ski boot clicking into a ski binding). LOOK also made the first carbon-fibre race-bike frames.

◀······· **A Tour de France rider on a LOOK bicycle**

Sports-clothing designer

Have you ever doodled a new kit for your favourite team? Maybe that was your first step to a career as a sports-clothing designer. Of course, this job is not just about kit that only looks good: it has to work well, too.

CLOTHING TECH

Sports-clothing designers need to understand the latest fabric technology. They pick the fabrics based on where and how the clothes will be used. A mountaineer on Everest, for example, needs clothing that is warm in freezing conditions and light to carry. The designer needs to understand physiology to understand the mountaineer's movements and how much they will sweat while climbing.

A climber on an indoor wall needs light, stretchy clothing that allows a wide range of movement.

WORLD OF SPORT

As a sports-clothing designer you could be involved in a huge range of activities. You might design wetsuits for surfing in sub-zero waters, heatproof suits for race-car drivers, breathable kit for football teams playing in hot countries or hi-tech swimming costumes for Olympic racers. Your sports kit will have to look good as well and may need to be bright to stand out, so you'll need to enjoy drawing and working with colour.

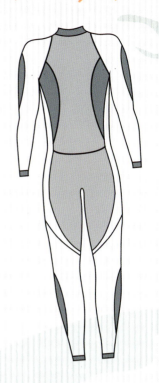

TESTING:
EXTREME TESTING

Adventure-sports companies test their new designs in extreme conditions. Their test engineers are usually fabric experts who are constantly reviewing new products. The test data they use comes from athletes using a prototype or early versions of the new products. They give feedback on how it fits, whether it works well and improvements that can be made.

Testing a new wetsuit will see how well it keeps a surfer warm in colder waters.

Race-car designer

Anyone who loves cutting-edge technology and fast cars will find their dream job in motorsports as a race-car designer. To create a winning car, you have to understand aerodynamics, motor design, suspension, materials technology and more.

CAD AND CAE

A lot of your work will be done on computers. Parts are designed using CAD, then virtually tested using CAE (short for 'computer-aided engineering'). CAE software can give you all kinds of information: how long an engine part should last, how a new body part should behave aerodynamically and even which suspension setting is likely to work best. This computer-based design process might produce 5,000 different parts before a new race car is first driven on a track.

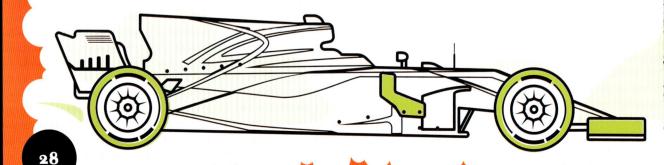

IRL

Of course, drivers don't race on computer screens (though they do practise on simulators). They race in real life – so that's where your designs will finally be tested. Many designers once worked as race engineers, who are a crucial part of a driver's pit crew (see pages 32–33). This gave them experience of different drivers, race types, tracks and conditions.

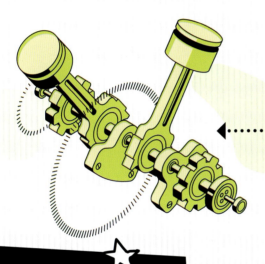

Race-car designers work on every single part of the car, including the mechanics found ················ inside the engine.

STEM STAR: ADRIAN NEWEY (1958–)

Adrian Newey is a legendary designer in Formula 1 and IndyCar. He studied aeronautics and astronautics at university, then went straight to work for the Fittipaldi Formula 1 team. He moved to the US CART race series, then back to Formula 1. He has designed cars for the Williams, McLaren and Red Bull teams and his cars have won more than 150 Grands Prix.

Behind the scenes:
NASCAR factory

A NASCAR factory is bursting with technology. During the racing season, everyone concentrates on making the team's cars as fast as possible. Once the season is finished, after everyone has a short holiday it is time to start working on next year's car.

CONSTANT DEVELOPMENT

All through the season, the factory works to improve its race car. Different teams work on power transmission, suspension, aerodynamics and how to use materials, such as carbon fibre. They try to make sure all the parts work together as well as possible.

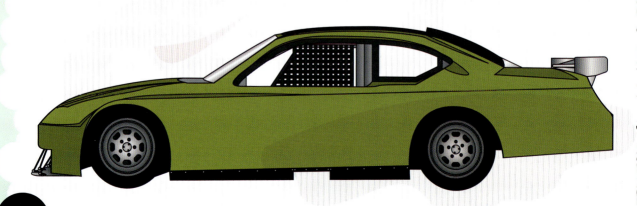

MACHINE SHOP

Designing new parts is no good if you can't manufacture them. In the machine shop, engineers work to produce the new parts, which are usually made of carbon fibre, metal or plastic. A new part can go from an idea in the designer's mind to an actual piece of the car in days – or sometimes hours.

WIND-TUNNEL TESTING

In the wind tunnel, the whole car's aerodynamic performance can be tested. Engineers can check, for example, how much downforce different wing angles produce at a variety of speeds. They can see whether new parts work as the CAE software predicted.

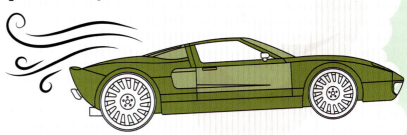

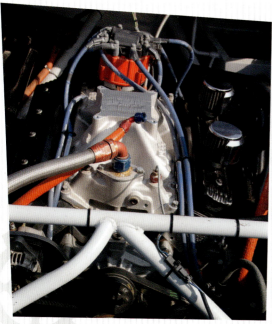

ENGINE AND GEARBOX TESTING

After the wind tunnel, this is the noisiest test area in the factory! Technicians run engines through a test process designed to check how long parts will last and how they work together. They also check the gearboxes to see how well they transmit power.

Motorsports pit crew

Can you imagine stepping out in front of a car that's travelling at 95 kph and trusting the driver to stop? If you can, perhaps you should aim for a job as a member of a race-team's pit crew.

RACE WEEKENDS

The pit crew is a group of the engineers and specialists that works on a car or bike at the races. Most important is the race engineer, who the driver talks to about problems with the car. The race engineer needs to understand the same race technologies as the driver: from aerodynamics to tyres, computer systems that control engine power, and suspension.

A NASCAR pit crew gets to work during .... a race.

Having graduated with a Master's degree in aerospace engineering, Gade went on to work with race teams in GT and endurance racing. In 2011, she became the first female race engineer to win the Le Mans 24 Hours race, before winning it again in 2012 and 2014. After a short stint in IndyCar, she moved into the Daytona Prototype International with Mazda.

◀ ····· Leena Gade talks to a pit crew member.

WORKING WEEKENDS

If you'd like a job where you get every weekend off, this may not be for you. On the other hand, if rebuilding a motorbike overnight after a crash in practice, living in hotels for half the year and being at every race sounds like your idea of fun, this could be a dream job. There are many different types of motorsports where the team needs a pit crew: MotoGP racing, rallying, Formula 1 and Nascar, for example.

Members of the Mercedes ····· team study data sent by their team's cars.

Film editor

Have you ever watched a film and wondered halfway through: 'What on Earth is going on? It's just become too hard to follow! Someone should have sorted this out.' Well, that someone was the film's editor.

TELLING TALES

As film editor, your job is turning hundreds, or even thousands of hours of footage into a story viewers will understand and enjoy. The editor often starts this process alone, then shares it with other people. If you don't like other people looking at your work and suggesting improvements, this probably isn't the right job for you!

SCREEN WORK

Film editors work on screen. (That sounds obvious, but years ago they used to work with actual film, cutting and linking sections together.) Editors put the scenes together in order, add different views, work out when the special effects need to be added and work out timings for the music and soundtrack. Most feature films are edited using software called Avid Media Composer, but Premiere Pro and Final Cut are also popular.

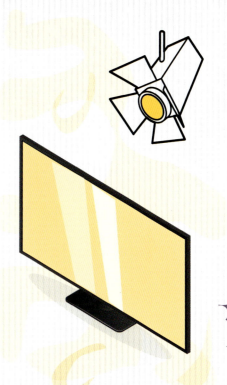

TRAINING:
BECOMING A FILM EDITOR

Start by editing your own videos at home using a cheap or free editing app, such as iMovie. Many editors then get their start by working as a runner – a general helper for film-production companies. This is a good way to meet people who might let you watch an edit happening. They may even be willing to let you get some work experience with a film company.

A film crew can contain a lot of different people. ·········▶

Behind the scenes:
Special effects

Film special effects are a big business. To create realistic effects, the film industry uses some of the very latest state-of-the-art science and technology, sometimes spending millions of pounds on a single scene! Today, many of these effects are made using computers. To work in special effects, you need scientific knowledge, ace computer skills and a wild imagination.

CGI EFFECTS

Computer-generated imagery (CGI) is added after filming. In action films, dramatic effects, such as explosions, are created using CGI, while whole characters are generated on computers for futuristic science-fiction films, such as *Star Wars*. CGI is also used to create realistic street scenes in dramas set in the past. The action is filmed in front of a green screen and the background is added later on by the special effects team.

DOLLY ZOOM

While most of the magic is added post-production, some special effects have to be made on-set. One common technique is known as the dolly zoom. The camera moves (dollies) towards or away from the subject at the same time as a lens zooms out or in. This has the effect of leaving a person the same size while the background around them rapidly shrinks or grows in size. First used in Alfred Hitchcock's 1958 film *Vertigo*, the dolly zoom has been employed in many famous films since, including *Jaws* and *The Lord of the Rings*.

.... **A camera is usually moved on a set of rails.**

STEM STAR:
RAY HARRYHAUSEN
(1920–2013)

Legendary US animator Ray Harryhausen invented a special effects technique called Dynamation. He used this technique to insert model monsters into pre-recorded scenes with live actors. Harryhausen's most famous Dynamation action sequence came in the 1963 film *Jason and the Argonauts*, in which three live actors battle with seven model skeletons. The models had to be painstakingly repositioned for each frame of film in a technique called stop motion. It took Harryhausen more than four months to complete the sequence.

Mobile surveillance officer

The job of a mobile surveillance officer is to watch other people without being noticed. They observe suspected criminals and terrorists, gathering information on what they are doing to help to stop crimes or terror attacks.

SPYING TECHNOLOGY

As a mobile surveillance officer, you will be a member of the security services and part of a team of people using a wide variety of technologies. Computers help to identify suspects: for example, they may use face-recognition and biometric software to process CCTV images. CCTV is also used to help keep track of suspects. Radio or mobile technology keeps the team members in touch with each other. You would also need to use high-tech camera and sound recording equipment.

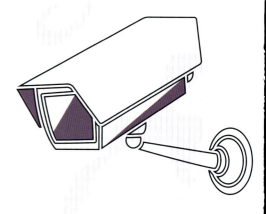

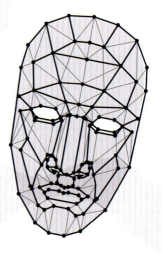

Facial recognition software .... checks key features on a person's face to identify them.

CONCENTRATION REQUIRED

This is a job that requires excellent concentration. You will probably be spending a lot of time sitting around doing nothing except watching. Then, suddenly, you have to spring into action: following a suspect on foot or even chasing them down. As a mobile surveillance officer you will have to blend into your surroundings. Things like having obvious tattoos or being very tall, which would make you stand out in a crowd, would probably mean you could not get this job.

TRAINING:
MOBILE SURVEILLANCE

The details of exactly how mobile surveillance officers are trained are kept secret. They have to learn surveillance skills, technical skills, such as operating radios, computers and cameras, and be fit enough to follow suspects on foot. At first officers learn through a combination of classroom lessons and real-life practice. Once their basic training is complete, they usually work with a mentor for at least six months.

Mobile teams will check in ....▶
with a central base.

Uniform designer

Lots of people wear uniforms, from police officers to soldiers, firefighters and of course schoolchildren. If you've ever spent time sketching out (or even just imagining) designs of a new kit for your school, maybe you're a budding uniform designer?

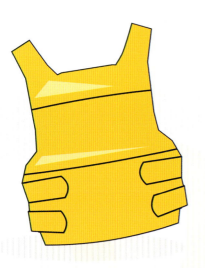

UNIFORM TECHNOLOGY

Whatever kind of uniform you are designing, understanding the latest technologies will be crucial. One of the most important is fabric technology. A police uniform, for example, will probably include some form of body armour. Firefighters need to wear heat-proof clothing. You also need to understand manufacturing technology, so that the uniform you design can actually be made. The design will be finalised on a computer, using specialist software.

WHERE TO WORK

There are lots of different kinds of uniform you could help design. Many people work for uniform-making companies. Some of these specialise in particular kinds of uniform, such as sports kit or hotel outfits. Technical uniforms, for example new uniforms for the armed forces or police, require lots of expertise as they have to cope with extreme conditions, such as the raging heat of a fire or a violent attack. They use a team of people, experts in different parts of the design, working together.

FAMOUS DESIGN:

THE TRENCH COAT

Today trench coats are a fashion item, but their history is much more interesting. During the First World War (1914–18), British officers became sick of their old-style woollen greatcoats, which became heavy with water and mud. Trench coats used gabardine instead of wool. This new fabric, invented by Thomas Burberry (1835–1926), was lightweight, waterproof and not too sweaty. The trench coat is still worn by many people today.

Aircraft designer

Imagine looking up one day as you hear an aircraft overhead and realising it's a plane you helped design. For that to happen you will need to become an aerospace engineer.

ENGINEERING FLIGHT

An aerospace engineer's key tool is a computer. This is not only used to design safe aircraft, but also to process the results of tests on new designs and materials. Of course, one person doesn't usually design a whole plane. Instead, teams of engineers work on different technologies. You could find yourself working on lightweight materials, wing design, jet engines, flight-control and computer systems, or low-emission engineering.

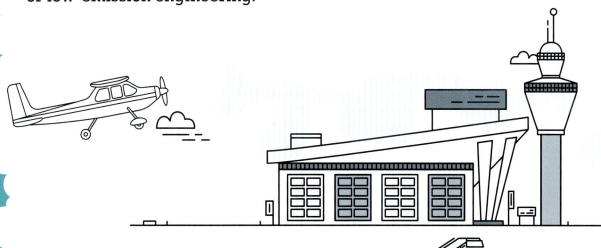

SMALL PLANES, LARGE PLANES

As an aircraft designer, safety is always a priority when developing new designs. With air travel set to increase in the coming years, other important design issues will be environmental:

- fuel efficiency: a small solar-powered plane has already flown around the world, but maybe you could design the first solar passenger plane?
- long distance: planes use a lot of fuel taking off and landing, so ones that can carry passengers a long way without stopping save fuel.
- electric planes, whether small personal-travel vehicles to larger passenger planes, do not burn fossil fuels.

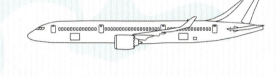

STEM STARS: WRIGHT BROTHERS
WILBUR (1867–1912), ORVILLE (1871–1948)

Wilbur (right) and Orville (left) Wright were bicycle-makers (as well as being clever mathematicians and engineers) who were fascinated by the idea of flying. They began designing and making aircraft. On 17 December 1903, their plane *Wright Flyer* made the first-ever powered flight.

Nuclear technician

How would you like to help control one of the most powerful events on Earth: the splitting of atoms? This releases huge amounts of energy – as well as deadly radiation – which it will be your job to monitor and control.

RADIATION ALERT

Most nuclear technicians work in power stations. Here your job is mainly to check that nuclear technology is running safely and well. Devices called dosimeters are used to record levels of radiation in power station staff, as well as in samples of the air, soil, rivers and ocean nearby. Nuclear technicians may also give their fellow workers advice on safety procedures.

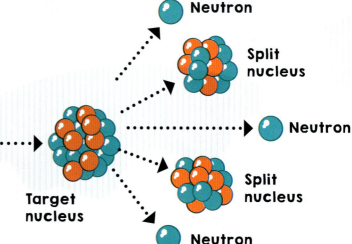

Neutron

Split nucleus

Neutron

Split nucleus

Neutron

Neutron

Target nucleus

Splitting atomic nuclei releases energy and more neutrons, which go on to split more nuclei in a chain reaction.

POWER AND MORE

In a power station, there are two main kinds of nuclear technician. Operating technicians are responsible for how well everything is working. They make changes, if needed, to the reactors and other equipment. Radiation-protection technicians are the ones who check radiation in the power station and surrounding area. This kind of technician sometimes works in nuclear-waste management, checking the safe disposal, recycling or storage of nuclear waste.

STEM STAR: NIELS BOHR
(1885-1962)

Bohr was one of the scientists who first explained the structure of atoms. During the Second World War (1939–45) he fled from Nazi Germany and helped the Allied forces develop nuclear weapons. For the rest of his life Bohr campaigned for the peaceful use of atomic energy and the sharing of nuclear technology.

Glossary

aerospace
technology and engineering of flight, both into space and through the air

air resistance
a force that pushes back against objects moving through a gas

app
short for 'application', a computer programme that is designed to do a particular job (such as checking the weather)

autism
condition that makes it difficult for people to communicate clearly, and also sometimes causes people to keep repeating the same behaviours over and over again

biometric
using statistics to understand how human bodies usually work and are shaped

CAD
short for computer-aided design

CCTV
short for closed-circuit television, a system of cameras and screens

used to watch streets, shopping centres, railway stations and other places

CT scanner
short for 'computerised tomography' scanner. These take X-rays from a variety of angles, then use computers to produce a series of images showing 'slices' of the body.

database
lots of data collected together in one place, where it can be accessed

defuse
make safe. When speaking about bombs, it literally means removing the fuse, the part of the bomb that sets it off.

diagnose
identify the cause of a problem. In medicine, diagnosing an illness means naming what is wrong with the patient.

DNA
deoxyribonucleic acid, a code that tells the body's cells how to grow

fabric
what something is made of and another word for cloth

fossil fuel
fuel formed from dead plants and animals that lived millions of years ago. Fossil fuels include coal, oil, gas and peat.

frame
in a bicycle, the frame is the central part that the wheels, seat, handlebars and pedals are attached to. Bike frames are usually made of metal, but are sometimes made of other materials, such as carbon-fibre or wood.

Grands Prix
name for major motor races involving specially designed powerful cars

IRL
short for 'in real life'

keyhole surgery
surgery performed through very small cuts in the patient's body, so that the surgeon's tools cause as little damage as possible

kidney
organ that filters out the body's waste products and sends them to the bladder in the form of urine (wee). Mammals usually have two kidneys.

leg splint
piece of something hard that can be tied to a broken or injured leg for support and strength

low-emission
releasing only small amounts of polluting gas

NASA
short for National Aeronautics and Space Administration, the organisation that runs the US space programme

para-athlete
athlete with a disability that makes them eligible to take part in the Paralympics

physicist
person who studies physics, the science of matter and energy

physiology
part of the science of biology, to do with how living things work

pit crew
group of people who work at a motorsports event to make sure the vehicle is race-ready

prototype
first or early version of a new product

radiation
energy travelling through space. Sunlight is a form of radiation: it is energy from the Sun that travels through space to Earth, where it powers our weather, warms the seas and provides us with warmth.

reactor
part of a nuclear power station where atoms are split to release huge amounts of energy

runner
general helper when a TV or film is being made. Runners usually earn little or nothing and are doing the job to get experience of the industry.

sample
small part of something that shows what the whole of it is like. For example, a skin sample is a tiny bit of skin that shows what the rest of a person's skin is like.

simulator
machine designed to reproduce a particular experience. For example, flight simulators reproduce the experience of flying a plane

ski binding
piece of ski equipment that connects the ski to the ski boot

software
instructions followed by a computer when it is doing tasks

spectrometer
device for measuring changes in radiation, energy or other things that change their strength

thermal
to do with heat

three-dimensional
showing height, width and depth

tumour
growth of a lump or swelling in the body, which is caused by cells reproducing themselves very quickly

two-dimensional
showing height and width, but not depth

welding
using heat to join together two objects or pieces of a material, usually metal

X-ray
form of electromagnetic energy, which can pass through soft body tissue, such as skin. An X-ray is also the resulting image.

Index